This book belongs to _9Delli Music_

Address _2249 Grant St_

Date _1989_

My own book of Prayers

Compiled by Mary Batchelor

Illustrated by Joy Barling Loyla,
Barrie Thorpe and Kathy Wyatt

A LION BOOK

Tring · Belleville · Sydney

Text and illustrations © 1984 Lion Publishing

Published by
Lion Publishing Corporation
10885 Textile Road, Belleville, Michigan 48111, USA
ISBN 0 85648 779 1

First edition 1984

Library of Congress Cataloging in Publication Data

Main entry under title:
My own book of prayers.

   1. Children–Prayer-books and devotions–English.
I. Batchelor, Mary.
BV265.M9 1984   242'.82   83-23897
ISBN 0-85648-779-1

Phototypesetting by Parkway Group, London and Abingdon
Printed and bound in Hong Kong
by Mandarin Offset International (HK) Ltd

Contents

ME

When we pray we talk to God. God is so great and wonderful that he can hear what we say to him even when we whisper. He made us, so he always knows just how we are feeling. Sometimes we kneel to pray, to remind us that God is the most important Person in the world as well as being our heavenly Father. We can shut our eyes to stop us looking at everything around us and to help us think about our prayers. God loves each one of us. He loves to listen when we talk to him.

Dear God, you are very great and wonderful.
Thank you for loving me and for promising
to listen when I talk to you.
Please be close to me now.
Amen

Dear Father, whom I cannot see,
I know that you are near to me.
Quite quietly I speak to you:
Please show me what you'd have me do.
Please help me plan kind things to do
For other people and for you.
Thank you for always helping me,
Dear Father, whom I cannot see.

Thank you, God, for making our world.
Thank you for all the good things
you have given to us.
Thank you for making me.
Help me to be happy and loving and kind.
For Jesus' sake.
Amen

God made the sun
And God made the tree,
God made the mountains
And God made me.

I thank you, O God,
For the sun and the tree,
For making the mountains
And for making me.

Something to do

Describe yourself by filling in the gaps:

My name is Kelli Music.

My hair is brown

My eyes are Drbrown

MY FAMILY *The Grown-ups*

God puts us in families so that we won't be lonely and so that children can be looked after. It may be Mom or Dad, Grandma or perhaps Aunt or Uncle who buys the food, washes the clothes, cooks the meals and takes care of us when we are ill. Some children have a new family to take care of them in place of their first Mom. We are glad to have grown-ups to take care of us. We say thank you to God for them all.

Thank you, God our Father,
For a Mom and a Dad,
For a Grandpa and Grandma;
For Aunts and Uncles,
For all grown-ups who take care of me
and make me feel safe,
Thank you, dear Father in heaven.

Thank you for my mother dear,
Always loving, always near;
Help me show in all I do
That I really love her too.

Now thank we all our God,
With hearts and hands and voices,
Who wondrous things has done,
In whom his world rejoices;
Who from our mother's arms
Has blessed us on our way
With countless gifts of love,
And still is ours today.

Something to do

In the space, write the names of the people who take care of you most of the time and ask God to bless them.

Mom   Grandma MoMo

MY FAMILY

Perhaps you have lots of brothers and sisters – or just one. If you are an only child, you may have cousins who come to play or stay with you. Jesus grew up in a family. He knows all about the fun, as well as the fights, that go on.

You can choose the prayers on this page that suit your family group.

Thank you, God, for my brothers and sisters.
Thank you for my big brother (sister)
who takes care of me and helps with things
that are too hard.
Thank you for all the fun we enjoy together.
Help us to take turns with favorite toys
and not to argue and fight.

Thank you, Lord Jesus, for our dear little baby.
Help me to be gentle with him
and not to mind when he gets extra attention.
Soon he'll be able to walk and talk
and we can play together.

Brothers, Sisters, Cousins

May the love of God our Father
Be in all our homes today;
May the love of the Lord Jesus
Keep our hearts and minds always:
May his loving, Holy Spirit
Guide and bless the ones I love,
Father, Mother, brothers, sisters,
Keep them safely in his love.

Something to do

In the space, write down the names of some of the
people in your family.

MY FAMILY

Jesus taught that everyone who loves and trusts him is made one of God's children and becomes part of God's big family all over the world. Jesus gave us a special family prayer, which we often say in church or at school. It reminds us that God is our Father. He wants us to love and trust him for everything and to love and forgive the other children in God's family.

The family prayer that Jesus gave to us:

Our Father in heaven:
May your holy name be honored;
may your kingdom come;
may your will be done on earth as it is in heaven.
Give us today the food we need.
Forgive us the wrongs we have done,
as we forgive the wrongs that others have done to us.
Do not bring us to hard testing,
but keep us safe from the Evil One.
For yours is the kingdom, and the power,
and the glory for ever.
Amen

Belonging to God's Family

Thank you, Father in heaven,
for making me your child through Jesus.
Thank you that everyone who loves you
is a brother or sister of mine.
Thank you for the family of Jesus
the whole wide world over.
Please make us all one.

Thank you, God,
for being my good, kind and loving Father.
Help me to be your obedient, kind
and loving child.
For Jesus' sake.
Amen

Something to do

Learn by heart this verse from the Bible
about being God's child:

'See how much the Father has loved us!
His love is so great that we are called
God's children.'

15

MY HOME

Jesus' home was in a town called Nazareth, where Joseph, Mary's husband, was the carpenter. I imagine Jesus often helped Mary in the house and ran errands for her and for Joseph. As he grew up he learned to be a carpenter too. He understands what it is like at home.

Thank you, God, for all the people
who come to our home:
for the delivery men,
for those who collect the garbage;
for neighbors who come to see us;
for friends who come to play.
Please make our home a happy place
for people to visit.

Take my hands, Lord Jesus,
Let them work for you,
Make them strong and gentle,
Kind in all I do;
Let me watch you, Jesus,
Till I'm gentle too,
Till my hands are kind hands,
Quick to work for you.

Thank you, Lord Jesus, for my home.
Thank you that it keeps me warm and dry
in all weather. Thank you for my bed;
thank you for my bath; thank you for the warm kitchen
where we can cook our meals.
Please be with all children who have no home.
Keep them safe and please give them
the shelter they need.
Amen

We thank thee, Lord, for all that thou dost give,
And for the happy homes in which we live:
For all the joy we have from day to day,
For all thy love, accept our thanks, we pray.

Something to do

Fill in your address: I live at _2249_

FloriDa

17

MY DAY Getting Up in the Morning

Some children (and grown-ups too!) find it hard to get up in the morning. But if you get out of bed just a minute or two earlier, you can start the day happily by thanking God for the night safely passed and asking him to bless the new day.

My Father, for another night
Of quiet sleep and rest,
For all the joy of morning light,
Your holy name be blest.

O Lord, for your keeping
While I was sleeping,
I thank you and pray,
Be with me today.

Dear Jesus, bless my hands
And all my playing:
Dear Jesus, bless my head
And all my thinking:
Dear Jesus, bless my feet
And all my running:
Dear Jesus, bless me all day long
And help in all I do.

Loving Father, all this day
Bless me in my work and play:
Bless the good I mean to do,
Help me do it, Lord, for you.
Bless the people I shall meet,
Give me loving hands and feet,
Quick to help them, quick to do
All I can for love of you.

Thank you, God, for giving us
another new day. Help me to enjoy my
work and my play. Help me to make it
a happy day for everyone else.
Amen

Something to do

On the clock, draw in the hands to point to
the time you get up on weekday mornings.

MY DAY *Mealtimes*

Many people in our world are hungry. How glad we are that we have food to eat! Jesus said 'thank you' to God, his Father, before he began meals. Everything we eat and drink comes from God, though lots of people work to make it ready for us.

Thank you for the world so sweet
Thank you for the food we eat,
Thank you for the birds that sing,
Thank you, God, for everything.

First the seed
And then the grain;
Thank you, God,
For sun and rain.

First the flour
And then the bread;
Thank you, God,
That we are fed.

Thank you, God,
For all your care;
Help us all
To share and share.

Bless, dear Lord, my daily food.
Make me strong and make me good.

Something to do

Write down your three favorite foods in the space and say thank you to God for them.

_____

_____

_____

MY DAY *Going to Bed*

God has taken care of us all through the day. Now it's bedtime, but God does not go to sleep. God takes care of us while we sleep and whenever we wake up he is near. He keeps us safe the whole night through.

Now the day is over,
Night is drawing nigh,
Shadows of the evening
Steal across the sky.

Through the long night-watches
May your angels spread
Their white wings above me,
Watching round my bed.

Jesus, tender Shepherd, hear me,
Bless your little lamb tonight;
Through the darkness please be near me.
Keep me safe till morning light.

Dear Lord, thank you for the darkness
that rests our eyes after the long day.
Now your sun is shining on the children
who live on the other side of the world.
Please bless their day, and bless our night.
Amen

Dear Father, when the light is out
and the house is quiet
and everyone else is asleep,
you are still close to me.
Help me to remember that I am safe
in your keeping the whole night through.
Amen

Glory to thee, my God, this night
For all the blessings of the light;
Keep me, O keep me, King of kings,
Beneath thy own almighty wings.

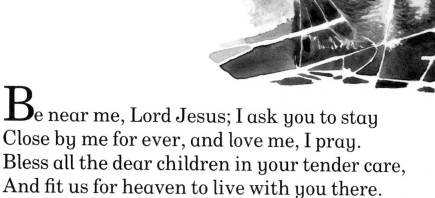

Be near me, Lord Jesus; I ask you to stay
Close by me for ever, and love me, I pray.
Bless all the dear children in your tender care,
And fit us for heaven to live with you there.

Something to do

On the clock, draw in the hands to point to
the time you go to bed during the week.

MY SCHOOL *In Class*

When Jesus was a boy he went to school, like us. As well as reading and writing, he had to learn a great many things by heart. He knows about the fun of learning and understands when we find classwork hard.

If Jesus had come as a boy to your school, he would not have worn clothes like yours, or known the games you play. So when boys and girls from other countries come to your school make friends with them and help them to feel they belong.

Father, bless our school today;
Be in all we do or say;
Be in every song we sing;
Every prayer to thee we bring.

Thank you, Lord,
for all the fun we have at school.
Thank you for bright crayons and paints,
for water and sand.
Thank you for picture books and reading books.
Thank you for music and singing and dancing.
Help us to enjoy ourselves at school today.

Dear Father,
Thank you for children from other lands
who come to my school.
Help us to learn from one another.
Teach me not to laugh at them because they
are different or to leave them to feel lonely.
Help me to make them my friends,
for Jesus' sake.

Let us praise the Father, who shows us, of his grace,
The secret paths of science, the mastery of space,
The wonder of computers, of TV, radio, trains,
For man made these, but God made man,
And God gave man his brains.

In our work and in our play,
Jesus, ever with us stay;
May we always strive to be
True and faithful unto thee.

Something to do

Write down the name of your school in the space. _____

MY SCHOOL *Out of Class*

Jesus is ready to help us whenever we need him – in lesson time, out in the playground, or when we are having school lunch. He will help us if we feel frightened or lost. He wants us to take care of the little ones and to make friends with lonely children.

Lord Jesus, please bless us
as we play at school today.
Help the big ones not to tease or bully.
Help the lonely ones to find friends.
Help the little ones to feel brave and safe.
Make our playtimes happy.

When we are tempted to be unkind,
When we are tempted to be unfair,
When to others' troubles we are blind,
Remind us how *we* would feel, and make us care.

Kind and loving Jesus
We ask that you will keep us
Kind and loving children
When we go out to play.
Help us to share our games,
Help us to play with children
Who need a friend today:
Help us to be gentle with the little ones:
Keep us kind and loving
In our play today:
Keep us kind and loving
All this happy day.

Something to do

Write down the name of your own teacher. ___Miss Hilton___

MY FRIENDS

Let's say thank you to God for our friends! Sometimes our friends are nice to us but at other times we quarrel. Jesus taught us to say we are sorry when we have been unkind and to forgive our friends when they have hurt us. Jesus had lots of friends and some special best friends too. Jesus will always be our best friend. He will never leave us or make us sad.

Jesus, Friend of little children,
Be a friend to me;
Take my hand and ever keep me
Close to thee.

Never leave me, nor forsake me,
Ever be my friend;
For I need thee from life's dawning
To its end.

Thank you for friends who play with me;
Thank you for friends who walk home with me;
Thank you for friends who live close to me.
Please make me a good friend too.

Dear Lord Jesus,
Help me to be a friend to others today.
When they are sad, help me to comfort them.
When they are lonely,
help me to play with them.
When no one likes them,
help me to be kind to them.
When they are frightened, help me
to stay close to them and make them brave.

Something to do

The name of one of my best friends is _____

MY PLAYTIME

*How many different ways there are to enjoy playtime!
Alone, or with friends; out of doors, indoors; in pretend
games, or with toys and books. There is never enough
time to do all the things we could. Let's think too of
children who are ill or handicapped and can't enjoy
some of our favorite games and play.*

For all the strength we have,
To run and leap and play,
For all our limbs so sound and strong,
We thank you, Lord, today.

Make all your children, Lord,
Healthy and strong like me,
To run and leap and shout and play,
And praise you in our glee.

Jesus, may I be like you;
Loving, kind in all I do;
Kind and happy when I play
Close beside you all the day.

For TV, radio, puzzles, books,
Thank you, Lord;
For teddy bears, for dolls and toys,
Thank you, Lord;
For bats and balls and roller skates,
Thank you, Lord;
For music, stories, fun and play,
Thank you, Lord.

Thank you, God, for playtime.
Thank you for my eyes – I can read
books and watch television programs.
Thank you for my ears – I can listen
to music and stories.
Thank you for my hands – I can paint,
cut out and make things.
Thank you for my legs –
I can run, skip and jump.
Thank you, God, for playtime.

Something to do

Today I played at

_____

MY WORLD *In the City*

Cities are exciting places. There is so much to see and to do. But they can be a bit frightening too. We can ask God to take care of us in the busy streets and stores, because our city is part of his world.

Thank you, Lord, for all the exciting things
to see in towns and cities.
Thank you for the bright store windows
and for the escalators inside.
Thank you for buses and cars and trains.
Thank you for museums and zoos,
for parks and playgrounds.
Thank you for all the fun of being in the city.

Please, God, bless our city
and all the people who work in it.
Thank you for the bus drivers
and the train drivers.
Thank you for the store keepers
and the park keepers.
Thank you for the policemen who help us
if we're lost.
Please bless them all.

Help us to care for our fine town
And never to throw litter down.
Show us the things that we should do
To keep it fit for others too.

God of all our cities,
Each alley, street and square,
Please look down on every house
And bless the people there.

Something to do

Stick a bus ticket or a museum ticket in this
space.

MY WORLD *In the Country*

Perhaps you live in the country, or you may go there for a day out or on your vacation. God has made everything beautiful and he has put us in charge of his world. We are to take care of the trees and flowers and growing things so that everyone can enjoy them. We can help the farmers, too, by closing gates and picking up any bottles or plastic bags that could harm their animals.

O God, our loving Father,
thank you for the beautiful world you have made.
Remind us sometimes just to stop and look
at all the lovely things around us.
In your world even the little
everyday things are special.

God who has made the daisies
And every lovely thing,
He will accept our praises
And hearken while we sing.

All things bright and beautiful,
All creatures great and small,
All things wise and wonderful,
The Lord God made them all.

Each little flower that opens,
Each little bird that sings —
He made their glowing colors,
He made their tiny wings.

The purple-headed mountain,
The river running by,
The sunset and the morning
That brighten up the sky.

He gave us eyes to see them,
And lips that we might tell
How great is God Almighty,
Who has made all things well.

Something to do

Pick a small flower or leaf and press it by putting it between two pieces of tissue and placing it inside a heavy book for a few days. When it is ready you can put a dab of glue carefully on one side, then stick it onto this page. You could stick in a tiny bird's feather instead.

MY WORLD *In All Weathers*

We often complain about the weather. Perhaps it's raining, and you had planned a picnic, or it's too hot or too cold to play outside. But we need different kinds of weather to make the crops grow and the flowers bloom. So we can thank God for sun and rain, wind and frost.

Praised be our Lord for the wind and the rain,
For clouds, for dew and air;
For the rainbow set in the sky above
Most precious and kind and fair.
For all these things tell the love of our Lord,
The love that is everywhere.

Thank you, God, for today's weather.
If it rains or if the sun shines,
if it snows or if it blows,
there are always good games to play
and things to enjoy.
So, thank you for today's weather.

Sunshine, sunshine,
God sends us sunshine:
Thank you, God, for sunshine
Everywhere!

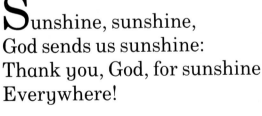

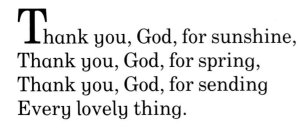

Thank you, God, for sunshine,
Thank you, God, for spring,
Thank you, God, for sending
Every lovely thing.

God sends the snow in winter,
The warmth to swell the grain,
The breezes and the sunshine,
And soft, refreshing rain.
All good gifts around us
Are sent from heaven above;
Then thank you, Lord, O thank you, Lord,
For all your love.

Something to do

Put a checkmark above the word that fits today's weather

Today it is: raining   sunny   windy   foggy   snowing   cloudy

MY WORLD *Animals*

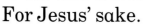

How many different kinds of animals there are in our world! Some are useful animals, like horses or sheep or guide dogs for the blind. Others make good pets. Some give us fun and make us laugh. Some are grand and terrible, like lions. God made them all and we can say thank you to him for each one.

Thank you for the beasts so tall,
Thank you for the creatures small.
Thank you for all things that live,
Thank you, God, for all you give.

Jesus said: 'Not one sparrow is forgotten by God.'

God, who takes care of the sparrows,
thank you for the birds that visit
our gardens and parks.
Teach me to be quiet
so that I can hear them singing
and let me help you to look
after them by giving them food
to eat and water to drink.
For Jesus' sake.
Amen

38

Loving Father, hear my prayer,
For all your creatures everywhere;
For animals both big and small,
And for my pets – please bless them all.

Something to do

Write down the name of your pet in this space
You can draw a picture of him on another piece of
paper. (If you have no pet of your own, write in the
name of the animal you would most like to own.)

_____

MY WORLD *The World Family*

*God made the children in every land. We may look
different, wear different clothes and speak different
languages, but God loves us all. He has no favorites.*

God saw that all things he had made
Were very very good,
He put us in this world of his
To live as children should.
To help each other, share and care,
To give, and love, and sing,
To work together for the good
Of every living thing.

Thank you, Father, for all the children we meet
who come to our country on vacation.
Thank you for school trips
when we can visit other lands.
Help the children of the world to learn
to know and love one another.
Amen

Our Father in heaven, we pray for
boys and girls in other lands.
Some are hungry,
some have no homes and some have no families.
Please be their loving Father
and take care of them all.
Amen

O God, who made the world
And all the people in it,
We remember in our prayers
Children of other lands,
For they are all your children.
We pray for boys and girls
Who never hear of you:
We pray that they may come to know
You are the loving Father
Of every girl and boy.

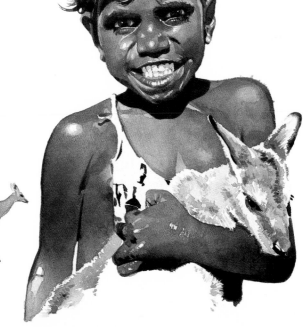

Something to do

Write down the name of a boy or girl you know about _____
who lives in another land. Ask God to bless
him or her today.

MY SAD DAYS

When Jesus was on earth he helped all kinds of ill people. When you are ill you can be sure that Jesus is especially close to you. Once you are up and about again, don't forget the children who are often ill and spend many days in bed or in the hospital.

Jesus, who healed the sick,
Be with me in my pain;
Please help me to be brave
And make me well again.

Jesus loves me, loves me still
When I'm very weak and ill;
From his shining throne on high
Watches with me where I lie.

When I am Not Well

Thank you, God, for all the people
who look after me when I am ill.
Thank you for Mom and Dad, Grandpa and Grandma.
Thank you for the doctor
who finds out what's wrong with me,
and the pharmacist who makes up the medicine.
Thank you for the nurses in the hospital
and the ladies who bring dinner around.
Please help me not to be grumpy and whine
because I have to stay in bed.

Dear Lord Jesus, when one of my friends
or someone in our family is ill,
help me to remember how it feels,
so that I know how to look after them
and cheer them up.
Amen

Something to do

Pray today for your busy doctor and for nurses in
hospital who take care of sick children.

43

MY SAD DAYS

Everyone is frightened sometimes. Some children are scared of dogs, others are afraid of the dark. When we pray we can tell Jesus just what it is that makes us frightened, even if we would not like to tell anyone else. He never thinks we are silly and he always understands.

Loving Shepherd of your sheep,
Keep your lamb, in safety keep;
Nothing can your power withstand,
None can pluck me from your hand.

Into thy loving care,
Into thy keeping,
Lord, who art everywhere,
Take us, we pray.

Lord Jesus,
when I am frightened and my heart beats fast,
help me to remember that you are very close to me.
Please make me brave and keep me safe.

Something to do

When Peter, one of Jesus' special friends, thought he was going to drown, he prayed a very short prayer, and Jesus heard and saved him. You can learn this prayer and say it when you are frightened. St Peter's prayer was: 'Save me, Lord!'

When I am Frightened

God the Father, bless us,
God the Son, defend us,
God the Spirit, keep us
Now and evermore.

MY SAD DAYS *When I Feel Lonely*

If you lose your teddy bear or your own special cuddly toy, you feel very miserable and unhappy. You feel very sad, too, if your pet dies or someone in the family goes away. They may only be away for a little while, but sometimes they go away and don't come back. Jesus wants us to share our sadness with him. He has promised, 'I will be with you always.' He never goes away.

Jesus is our childhood pattern:
Day by day like us he grew;
He was little, weak and helpless;
Tears and smiles like us he knew:
And he feels for all our sadness,
And he shares in all our gladness.

The God of love my shepherd is,
And he that does me feed:
While he is mine, and I am his,
What can I want or need?

Lord Jesus, please be with me on this sad day.
Thank you for the people who are trying to cheer me up.
Thank you that you love and understand me.
You are close to me all the time.
Thank you that happy days will come again.
Amen

Something to do

When one of his special friends died, Jesus was so
sad that he cried. If someone you love has gone
away for a little while, or even for ever, you can fill
in their name and pray like this: Dear Lord Jesus,
you understand how sad I am without _____
Please help me.

MY SAD DAYS *When I am Naughty*

When we are naughty, we always end up by being sad too. Worst of all, our naughtiness makes God sad, because it means that we have disobeyed him. But God loves us so much that Jesus, God's Son, came to our world and died to take our punishment. When we have done wrong and are really sorry, we can tell God about it. We can ask him to forgive us and make us good again, and he will. If we have made someone else unhappy, God will help us to say we are sorry.

There is a green hill far away,
Outside a city wall,
Where the dear Lord was crucified,
Who died to save us all.

He died that we might be forgiven,
He died to make us good,
That we might go at last to heaven,
Saved by his precious blood.

Thank you, dear Lord Jesus,
for taking my punishment.
You suffered pain and death
because you love me so much.
I am sorry that I have been naughty.
Please forgive me and help me to love
and please you.
Amen

For the things that I've done wrong,
Things that I remember long,
Hurting friends and those I love,
I am very sorry God.

Dear Father, help me to be kind,
And help me to be good;
Help me today to tell the truth,
And do the things I should.

Forgive me, Lord, for thy dear Son,
The ill that I this day have done,
That with the world, myself, and thee,
I, ere I sleep, at peace may be.

MY SPECIAL HAPPY DAYS *Sunday*

*Sunday is a special happy day for praising God and
learning more about him in church and Sunday
school. It's a day for being with our family and friends,
too.*

Sing to the Lord, all the world!
Worship the Lord with joy;
Come before him with happy songs!
The Lord is God.
He made us, and we belong to him;
We are his people, we are his flock.
Give thanks to him and praise him.
The Lord is good.

We have so much to thank you for,
Our heavenly Father dear:
For life and love and tender care,
Through all the happy year;
For homes and friends and daily food,
Each one a gift of love.
For every good and perfect gift
Is from our God above.

Dear Father, please make Sunday a happy day
when we can sing and talk to you
and learn to love you more.
Thank you for our church.
Help me to make you happy today
and to make my family happy, too.
For Jesus' sake.
Amen

50

Help our lips to praise you;
Help our hands to serve you;
Help our hearts to love you.

God be in my head, and in my understanding;
God be in mine eyes, and in my looking;
God be in my mouth, and in my speaking;
God be in my heart, and in my thinking;
God be at my end, and at my departing.

MY SPECIAL HAPPY DAYS

On Christmas Day we remember the birthday of the Lord Jesus, when he was born as a human baby into our world. When it's your turn to be the birthday boy or girl, you are special and important. Christmas is happiest for everyone when we remember that Jesus is the most important person in the whole exciting holiday and put him first.

Christmas

Baby Jesus, sleeping softly
On the warm and fragrant hay,
Children all the wide world over
Think of you on Christmas Day.

Dear Lord Jesus,
This is your birthday
and we bring you the gift of our love.
Thank you for the presents we give
and receive on your birthday.
Make our homes happy places
because we are all pleasing you
on your special day.

Jesus, Baby Jesus,
Mother Mary loves you,
Rocks you to sleep.

Jesus, Baby Jesus,
Shepherds run to find you,
Leaving their sheep.

Jesus, Baby Jesus,
Wise Men come to find you:
A star leads the way.

Jesus, Baby Jesus,
All the children love you,
Love Christmas Day.

Dear Lord Jesus,
You were born in a dirty stable with no
warm clean blankets or comfortable bed.
Please take care of babies and children
who are cold or hungry or alone
this Christmas time.
Help us to share our good things with them
so that they know that you love them too.

Something to do

You can sing your own favorite carol about
Jesus, in honor of his birthday.

MY SPECIAL HAPPY DAYS *Easter*

Easter is a time of sadness and of happiness. We are sad because Jesus died on Good Friday, but we are glad he died so that we could be forgiven and become God's friends. Easter Sunday is full of joy because God made Jesus alive again on that first Easter Day, and he is alive today and for always. Jesus has won the fight against evil and darkness and death in the whole world.

GOOD FRIDAY

It is a thing most wonderful,
Almost too wonderful to be,
That God's own Son should come from heaven,
And die to save a child like me.

Lord Jesus, you suffered pain and hurt for us;
you died on the cross to take away our sin.
Thank you for loving us so much.
Help us to love you too.

EASTER DAY

Lord Jesus, you are alive!
Thank you for winning the battle against death
and coming back to life, never to die again.
You are close to us now and for ever.
Thank you, Lord Jesus,
for the happiness of Easter Day.

Come, you children, sing to Jesus
On this happy Easter Day,
'Christ, our Savior, now is risen,'
Let his little children say.
All the bells are gladly ringing,
All the flowers are gaily springing,
All the birds with joy are singing;
Come, you children, praise and pray.

Jesus lives! for us he died;
Then, alone to Jesus living,
Pure in heart may we abide,
Glory to our Savior giving.

MY SPECIAL HAPPY DAYS

Birthdays are fun. There are cards and presents and sometimes a party. We want to say thank you to God for them all and for the kind people who have given them. As we think back to the last birthday we thank God for all the good things and for taking care of us all the time. We look ahead to an exciting new year of life and ask God to be with us the whole way through, whatever happens. We can be sure he will!

Comes a birthday once again,
Happy day, O happy day!
Through the sunshine, through the rain,
God has brought us on our way.

Father, let the new year be
Bright and holy, sweet and true;
Keep us always close to thee,
Day by day our whole life through.

Happy, happy birthday!
Happy year begun!
God, who gives us birthdays,
Knows them every one;
God is kind and loving,
He is sure to hear;
So we ask his blessing
For another year.

Birthdays

Teach us, dear Lord, to give and to share
so that we make each other's birthdays happy too.

Here is a Bible prayer for a birthday child:

May the Lord bless you and take care of you;
May the Lord be kind and gracious to you;
May the Lord look on you with favor
and give you peace.

Something to do

Fill in the space with the right number: This birthday I am _____ years old.

MY SPECIAL HAPPY DAYS

Sometimes we spend vacations at home, especially in winter, and enjoy playing with toys and with friends. In the summer we may go away for the day or go to stay with relatives. Sometimes we go to faraway places for a special vacation. Whatever we do and wherever we go, God is with us. He is glad when we are thankful and happy on our vacation and when we try to make others happy too.

Dear God, please take care of us when we go away on our vacation. Thank you for the excitement of the journey, for new places to see and new people to meet. Thank you, too, for the happiness of coming home when the vacation is over.

Thank you, Lord, for the fun of days out. Thank you for trips to the seaside. Thank you for picnics in the country. Thank you for visits to new towns and cities. Please give us happy vacations.

Vacations

Praise God from whom all blessings flow;
Praise him, all creatures here below;
Praise him, above, you heavenly host;
Praise Father, Son, and Holy Ghost.

Here is a Bible prayer that is just right for the end of the day – for the end of the vacation – and for the end of this book!

May the grace of the Lord Jesus Christ, the love of God and the fellowship of the Holy Spirit, be with us all, evermore. Amen

Acknowledgements

We would like to thank all those who have given us permission to include their prayers in this book, as indicated on the list below:

Church Information Office Publishing:
H. Widdows, p. 36, *Thank you God* from *In Excelsis*.

Concordia Publishing House Ltd:
Page 24, *Father, bless our school today* from *Little Folded Hands*.

Gerald Duckworth & Co. Ltd.:
Elizabeth Goudge, p. 36, *Praised be our Lord* from *Thanksgiving for the Earth*.

Lutterworth Press:
Leah Gale, p. 9, *God made the sun*; p. 40, *God saw all things he had made* from *Children's Prayers and Praises*.

Miss Nancy Martin:
Page 8, *Dear Father* and p. 25, *Let us praise the Father* from *Prayers for Young People and Children*.

A. R. Mowbray & Co. Ltd.:
Joan Gale Thomas, p. 33, *God of all our cities* from *God of all things*.

National Christian Education Council:
Lilian Cox, p. 21, *First the seed*; Florence Hoatson, p. 56, *Happy, happy birthday* from *New Child Songs*. Frederick A. Jackson, p. 56, *Comes a birthday* from *Child Songs*. Hilda Dodd, p. 52, *Baby Jesus, sleeping softly*.

New American Library of World Literature:
Phyllis Ohanian, p. 49, *Dear Father help me to be kind*.

Oxford University Press:
Margaret Kitson, p. 13, *May the love of God our Father*; p. 19, *Loving Father*; p. 27, *Kind and loving Jesus*; p. 41, *O God who made the world* from *Infant Prayer*.

Miss A. M. Pullen:
Page 53, *Jesus, baby Jesus* from *Infant Praise*.

Fleming H. Revell Co./The Seabury Press:
Page 51, *Help our lips to praise*.

Hilary Sanders:
Page 10, *Thank you for my mother dear* from *Infant Praise*.

Scripture Union:
Page 16, *We thank thee Lord* from *C.S.S.M. Choruses*.

The Seabury Press:
Norman and Margaret Mealey, p. 49, *For the things that I've done wrong* from *Sing for Joy*.

SPCK:
Eleanor Martin: p. 19, *Dear Jesus, bless my hands* from *Prayer and Praise in the Sunday Kindergarten*. Mrs Rutter Leatham, p. 20, *Thank you for the world so sweet*; M. Ensor, p. 30, *Jesus, may I be like you* from *Hymns and Songs for Children*.

Mr and Mrs J. Young:
Page 26, *When we are tempted to be unkind* from *Praying with Juniors*.

Bible quotations are from the *Good News Bible*, copyright 1966, 1971 and 1976 American Bible Society, published by the Bible Societies/ Collins

Every effort has been made to trace and contact copyright owners. If there are any inadvertent omissions in the acknowledgements we apologize to those concerned.